The Bust in Dust...

The Bust in Dust...

And other pick-me-up pearls
for when wisdom is waning

GK Kingsley

First published in 2014

Copyright © 2014 GK Kingsley

The Bust in Dust...

Text by GK Kingsley
Illustrations by GK Kingsley

The right by GK Kingsley to be identified as the author, originator and creator of this work has been asserted by her in accordance with the Copyright, Designs and Patents Act 1988.

All rights reserved. No part of this publication may be reproduced, stored or introduced into a retrieval system, or transmitted, in any form or by any means (electronic, mechanical, photocopying, recording or otherwise), without the prior written permission of both the copyright owner and the publishers of this book. Any person who does any unauthorized act in relation to this publication may be liable to criminal prosecution and civil claims for damages.

ISBN-10: 1500989312
ISBN-13: 978-1500989316

The Bust in Dust...

What others are saying about GK Kingsley...

"GK Kingsley writes for fun... her own and her reader's. But as you chuckle, you'll discover precious gems of wisdom and electric sparks of wit and insight in GK's deceptively simple rhyming verses. She magically transforms the commonplace into the extraordinary, and she may well have invented a new genre along the way: Post-it Poetry. I can't resist the urge to scribble down her regular short offerings and stick them around my desk, on the fridge, above my computer, until I know them by heart. It has been a delight to get to know this remarkable lady and her work over recent years." **Neil Marr. Fiction Editor. Monaco, France**

"I do love waking up to GK's daily verse - most times they could have been written just for me..." **Jaqui Somers. UK**

"GK Kingsley is a wonderful writer of verse. Her ability to make you smile is second to none. You can't help but appreciate the wit behind the words and her message of positivity always. She encourages you to laugh at yourself, the world, and all in it that tries us. It is often said, 'If you don't laugh you cry'... well thanks to GK Kingsley laughing is easy." **Heather Pennicott, New Zealand**

"GK's Scribblings always have me nodding in agreement whilst chuckling about all that life throws at us. An absolute gem." **Sam Milns, UK**

"I cannot remember the number of times I laughed out loud while in danger of spilling my coffee. GK's unexpected conclusions to wholly mundane issues are deeply amusing." **Jackie Keswick, UK**

"I love reading GK's work: Ranging from lively and fun to occasionally positively profound, but always thought-provoking, a GK Kingsley poem is just the daily tonic one needs!" **Gavin Orr, Scotland**

"Have you written any about me?..." **GK's son, Planet Football**

"Have you written any about me?!..." **GK's husband, Planet Patience**

The Bust in Dust...

AN IMPORTANT WORD OF THANKS...

A very BIG thank you to the dear friends and family who have encouraged and supported me over the years. Writing is my passion. And at times, when I've lost sight of what I'm doing, you've - quite simply - not let me stop. Thank you one and all. You know who you are...

The Bust in Dust

I confess to having moments
Of unplanned OCD
When bonds are forged with cleaning tools
Till they're at one with me
And in those vexing moments
I fear that I've matured
But then I draw some boobs in dust
And think, "Thank God! I'm cured."

© GKKingsley.com

The Bust in Dust...

Topping & Tale-ing

When chatting at a party
As my glass was being topped up
The question of 'How many?'
Was a topic that cropped up
And 'cos my glass had always
Just been topped as I conversed
I felt it only fair to answer
"Oh... I'm on my first!"

© GKKingsley.com

The Bust in Dust...

The Posturing Posterior

When dealing with an ostrich
In a battle of the wits
Be warned, they'll hide their head in sand
To air their thinking bits!

© GKKingsley.com

The Bust in Dust...

Chic Freak

I once was concerned I was freaky
And craved to like popular stuff
But when told to dazzle
I'd need a vajazzle
I figured new pants were enough

© GKKingsley.com

The Bust in Dust...

A Grave Message

It's true my home's untidy
And ironing mountains loom
From time to time I'll have a blitz
To clear some more leg room
My problem is my passion, see
I must pursue my dream
If life's sweet gift's a one off chance
To chase it rules supreme
And if one day my legacy
Is not quite as I planned
So what? I will have learnt a lot
And passed it on first hand
My mind will still rest easy
That I clung onto my vow
For I've never seen a gravestone say
'Here lies a messy cow...'

© GKKingsley.com

Mini de Me

I have reached that stage in life
When certain things appall
Like a twelve year old who answers back
And thinks he knows it all
Now I know that this is nothing new
For patience is the key
But the thing that's so unnerving
Is he sounds a lot like me!

© GKKingsley.com

The Bust in Dust...

Cheers to Tears!

We deck ourselves in jewellery
As a mark of our success
And craft a grand exterior
To stand out and impress
But the things that make us special
Are the gems ignored by fools
Like the tear drops of compassion
Which are Mother Nature's jewels

© GKKingsley.com

The Bust in Dust...

The Derma Squirmer

Delicate or wispy
Lissom, slight or slim
Willowy or lanky
Small, petite or trim
Not words I'm over fond of
They're more sweary-Mary spin
But I'd say I'm pretty skinny
'Cos I've got ALOT of skin!

© GKKingsley.com

The Bust in Dust...

A Thought for Darwin...

If early birds wake up for what
Dawn offers on a plate
You'd think that evolution
Would mean worms sleep in quite late

© GKKingsley.com

The Bust in Dust...

Losing Weight?

*Losing weight...
What's the scoop?
Some parts tone
Whilst others droop!*

© GKKingsley.com

The Bust in Dust...

The Cosmology of Drinking

I think my head has a wormhole
Undiscovered in astro reports
For when I drink
My brain expands
'Till there's infinite space between thoughts

© GKKingsley.com

The Bust in Dust...

Homework time – THE WAR ZONE
Tempers frayed and charred
Impressive dodging strategies
Put each side on its guard
So far he hasn't noticed
That my brain has turned to lard
But how long can I hide the fact
It's me who finds maths hard?!

Homework Irk

© GKKingsley.com

The Bust in Dust...

Spot the Difference...

So... when are not pants hot pants?
When they stretch from butt to tummy?
And look like quite a lot pants
That you'd see worn by your mummy?

And... when are hot pants not pants?
When they're sexy, saucy shorts?
That look like you forgot pants
With your mind on other thoughts...

© GKKingsley.com

The Bust in Dust...

Caprice in Peace

Some say that they are mindful
To get time on their own
The peaceful isolation
Realigns them in life's zone
Which makes me somewhat quirky
(A fact that's quite well known)
'Cos I just like to boogie
With my hairbrush microphone!

© GKKingsley.com

The Bust in Dust...

Social Media – The Bottom Line

I know that some are dubious
About this Facebook lark
And Twitter often leaves them cold
There is no LinkedIn spark
    I've also heard it quoted
    Interaction is by choice
    And all this social media
    Gives everyone a voice
But when my son found YouTube
All such logic fell apart
For ten year olds just go hi-tech
To watch folks light a fart

© GKKingsley.com

The Bust in Dust...

Puzzling Guzzling...

Last night we had some drinkies
And I'm not a-one for countin'
But let's just say the empties pile
Is more an empties mountain
But that's not what's perplexing
'Cos I like to play the host
No... What confounds is why
I also ate a ton of toast!

© GKKingsley.com

The Bust in Dust...

Eco Sucker

I declare I play my part
In this global warming war
For to save on washing up
I've swapped my wine glass for a straw!

© GKKingsley.com

De-Fence

With new ideas about to fledge
One hits a wall, a doubt-shaped edge
Which as the bricks and mortar bond
Dishearten, so few peer beyond
Yet boundaries are nothing more
Than mental decor to ignore
For limitations in the mind
Themselves are what should be confined

© GKKingsley.com

The Bust in Dust...

Double Trouble
(A Bird's Eye View)

My dearest darling hubby
When I'm stubborn and headstrong
Just know I can't agree with you
'Cos then we'd both be wrong

© GKKingsley.com

The Bust in Dust...

The Post-Booze Excuse...

Oh, those naughty little things you do
That make your stomach churn
"Not again!" You swear, next day
As wisdom does return
It's said regrets are pointless
If mistakes mean lessons learned
Ooopps! Doesn't touch a drop mid-week's
A badge I've yet to earn...

© GKKingsley.com

The Bust in Dust...

A Chatter Matter...

Some people love to chatter
They clearly like their voice
They want to share it with the world
Give man nor beast a choice
But chatter domination
Then means none can let them know
That to hold a conversation
At some point they must let go...

© GKKingsley.com

The Bust in Dust...

Your Saucy Look...

*When he hints he's horny
But you can't face the bother
Give him your most saucy look
And speak just like your mother*

© GKKingsley.com

The Bust in Dust...

Dear Santa, I'm worried...

When I hit forty
I'll look at my stocking
And think of the fun I have missed

So...

I'd rather be naughty
Perhaps even shocking...
And hereby resign from your list

© GKKingsley.com

The Bust in Dust...

L'amour de flaw(s)

Nature's imperfections
Are the things that catch the eye
Order without symmetry
Patterned yet awry
And I stand and stare straight upwards
At the vastness high above me
And I realise not being perfect
Gives a person space to love me...

© GKKingsley.com

The Bust in Dust...

Master Chef

Stewed haricot
Tomatoes and spice
Plus light muscovado
All served with a slice
Of crusty ciabatta
A meal one can boast
Is almost as tasty
As baked beans on toast

© GKKingsley.com

The Bust in Dust...

New Resolutions?

New resolutions?
Always troubling
Kept mine simple:
STOP BUTT WOBBLING!

© GKKingsley.com

The Bust in Dust...

En Garde!

I have a theory much pleasure is built
On double-edged swordplay, close quartered with guilt
For things that are treats, like chocolate and wine
Enjoy extra kudos 'cos we SHOULD decline
The measure of pleasure and guilt that is built
You'll find entwined to the tilt of the hilt
So all I can say, as blades twang with a clang
Blood will spill from your thrills, so bulk buy Cillit Bang!

© GKKingsley.com

The Bust in Dust...

One of a kind...

We all have our weak little moments
When another's opinion cuts deep
You know self-esteem should be self-regulated
But still you've collapsed in a heap
As you judge the extent of your value
Whilst your soul's feeling ravaged and lifeless
Never forget that there's only ONE you
And it's not that you're worthless... you're priceless!

© GKKingsley.com

The Bust in Dust...

Problem shared when vision's impaired...

When I think I've lost my bottle
Seen hopes blur as each sec passes
My bestest pal reminds me
I just need a pair of glasses!

© GKKingsley.com

To the male of our species...

When your nose is stuffy
And the shivers do abound
You're coughing up for England
And a headache starts to pound

Grab a piece of paper
Write your eulogy adieu
'Cos on your gravestone it will say
"He only had man-flu!"

© GKKingsley.com

The Bust in Dust...

Beauty Regime?

Beauty regime?
Kept mine simple:
Got foundation
Covered pimple...

© GKKingsley.com

The Bust in Dust...

Knowing your onions...

I've now become an onion
It is that time of year
I wear so many layers
What's the real me is unclear
But this metaphor's quite apt
And my sense of humour's tickled
For if I'm not a deep fried ring
I'm more than likely pickled!

© GKKingsley.com

The Bust in Dust...

The Meaning of Life

The meaning of life
Is hard to define
But I'm sure it's related
To chocolate and wine!

© GKKingsley.com

The Bust in Dust...

Double Trouble
(A Guy's Eye View)

Just know, dear darling wifey
When you're stubborn and headstrong
Our disagreeing pains me
'Cos I hate to know you're wrong

© GKKingsley.com

The Bust in Dust...

Is love all thrills and spills and fun
And feeling you're the only one?   **Love...**
Or does more loom when that is done?
To twist and bind the prize you've won
        A patient sigh, reply, a smile
        A kindness that is versatile
        A loyalty to face the trial
        Of life and all that can defile
Those plying strings to fend off foes
A bobbin there to share your woes
And you, a fleece for their repose
To counter sadness, juxtapose
        No, love's not thrills and spills and fun
        But more a lifelong yarn that's spun

© GKKingsley.com

The Bust in Dust...

A Shaky Sham?

If Friday's tempting yardarm
Prompts, "Shall I have a glass?..."
Does it make my Mon-Thursday angst
More... or less... a farce?

© GKKingsley.com

The Bust in Dust...

How to deal with a chancer...

If a bloke says you're one in a million
Take a hint from a lottery tip
He may think he's got to be in it to win it
And you're just his next lucky dip

When his thunderballs then start a-rollin'
And he asks if his luck's got a shot
Say no four-leaf clover will make you rollover
You'd rather a bigger jackpot!

© GKKingsley.com

The Bust in Dust...

Raise your glass to progress!

For me, the world of camping
Once a thing to be endured
Has taken on a different slant
Now that I've matured
For though we all forget things
Even when we make a list
The launch of screw-top bottles
Means a corkscrew's now not missed!

© GKKingsley.com

The Bust in Dust...

Tired or Inspired?

At times I think men's bodies
Are lacking in mystique
They have this dangly extra bit
Which ain't what you'd call sleek
I guess God had forgotten
That men also need a leak
And stuck it on last minute
Having done a six day week...

© GKKingsley.com

The Bust in Dust...

Juries & Prudence

It sometimes seems impossible
To get your point of view
Across that gaping gender gap
It comes out all askew
You try some different angles
But no matter what you say
He states that you're emotional
And logic holds most sway
Well, just one time that may apply
So rein in all your fury
'Cos claiming that 'IT' just fell off
Will not convince a jury....!

© GKKingsley.com

The Bust in Dust...

Hangovers

Hangovers are often just groggy
Tho' sometimes they also feel sore
But the worst ones of all
Are when I can't recall
Why the best place to sleep was the floor!

© GKKingsley.com

The Bust in Dust...

A Mug for a Hug

We all have our problems
Some long term, some short
It's not that we're needy
A drain on support
For really we're able
To fix any muddle
But, boy, do we welcome
A nicely timed cuddle

© GKKingsley.com

The Rhythm of the Evening

He breathes in, he breathes out
I am left in no doubt
That my darling's
Not yet kicked the bucket
But with just one more snore
Things will change on that score
'Cos I'll chop off his head
And think F##k it!

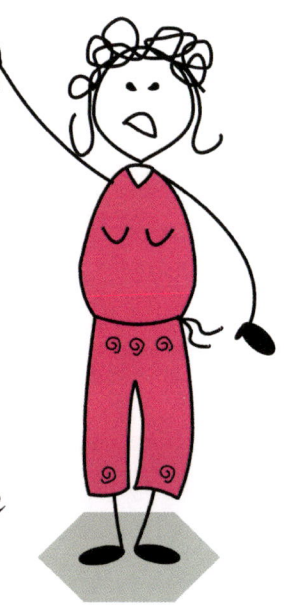

The Bust in Dust...

De-Cant...

When life seems unfulfilling
An irksome, mottled cup
I go and pour a glass
'Cos things are best not bottled up!

© GKKingsley.com

The Bust in Dust...

The shape of things to come...

One step forward, two steps back
Three steps sideways, way off track
A hop, a skip, a lunge, a dart
And, lo, you're right back near the start
So how does one break out this cycle?
Stop those folk who take the Michael?
Grow some wings? Reject their rules?
Refuse to tread their road for fools?
    Blame not those folk! Blame not the road!
    Blame not the boots you've been bestowed!
    Blame not your lack of winged estate!
    Blame your assumption roads are straight...

© GKKingsley.com

The Bust in Dust...

Replete and Sweet...

There is nothing sweeter
Than revenge that's been surpassed
For you realise they're not worth it
And you really can't be arsed...

© GKKingsley.com

The Bust in Dust...

A Droll Goal

I was told that with some focus
One can get where one aspires
One can be just what one wants to be
Have all that one desires
So feeling tired of being a lass
All feminine and frail
I thought that I would have a stab
At being an 'adult male'
At first it seemed to go quite well
But as the months then wore on
I discovered it's impossible
To be an oxymoron...

© GKKingsley.com

The Bust in Dust...

You know you're getting on when...

I'm worried I've hit middle age
For today I had my first clue
I discovered that pubes are not trendy
And teabagging isn't a brew!

© GKKingsley.com

The Bust in Dust...

You are what you eat...

As the years pass over
And everything heads south
I've heard one's health is coloured
By what's put inside one's mouth
So if my droops are grapey pink
From mixing reds and whites
Do you think they need a sticker
Saying, 'May contain sulphites'?

© GKKingsley.com

The Bust in Dust...

Talkin' out their...

Our lives are based on crossroads
Even when we breathe and swallow
Choosing airways or digestion
Things just know which route to follow
But when it comes to talking
Many override the pharynx
So the end of their digestive tract
Becomes a second larynx...

© GKKingsley.com

The Bust in Dust...

A BIT ABOUT GK KINGSLEY

GK Kingsley does have another existence. She would definitely prefer to spend most of her time as GK, but 'real life' gets in the way... It's a needing-to-eat-and-have-a-roof thing. But that's by the by... When GK's being GK, she writes bits of Post-it poetry, as well as full length fiction, and publishes new pieces regularly on her website (www.gkkingsley.com).

She also appears regularly on BBC Radio Northampton, summarising the week's events and news in a fun and lively poem. Occasional other ad hoc appearances boost her spirits too.

The Bust in Dust...

VISIT WWW.GKKINGSLEY.COM

GK loves connecting with people online, either via her website, Facebook, Twitter, LinkedIn or Pinterest. And if you'd like to receive her 'Latest Scribblings' weekly email update, you can subscribe to her mailing list via her website. She'll also keep you updated on new releases and announcements. Please do seek her out and connect with her. She doesn't bite!

GIVE IT!

GK is delighted to let you in on a secret: She now has a collection of mugs, coasters and... well... all sorts, really... you know... the kind of stuff that folk like to give to a friend. From boozy banter to life's little thought provokers, you can now have a dose of her humour and wit in your home. Just visit her website for more details. www.gkkingsley.com.

Made in the USA
Charleston, SC
18 September 2014